Free Verse Editions

Edited by Jon Thompson

WE'LL SEE

POEMS BY GEORGES L. GODEAU

Translated by Kathleen McGookey

Parlor Press
Anderson, South Carolina
www.parlorpress.com

Parlor Press LLC, Anderson, South Carolina, 29621

Translation of *We'll See* © 2012 by Parlor Press. All rights reserved.
We gratefully acknowledge Mme Madeleine Godeau, who granted permission to translate *We'll See* into English.

Cet ouvrage publié dans le cadre du programme d'aide à la publication bénéficie du soutien du Ministère des Affaires Etrangères et du Service Culturel de l'Ambassade de France représenté aux Etats-Unis.

This work received support from the French Ministry of Foreign Affairs and the Cultural Services of the French Embassy in the United States through their publishing assistance program.

Printed in the United States of America
S A N: 2 5 4 - 8 8 7 9

Library of Congress Cataloging-in-Publication Data

Godeau, Georges L.
  [On verra bien. English]
  We'll see : poems / by Georges L. Godeau ; translated by Kathleen McGookey.
      p. cm. -- (Free verse editions)
  Translation of On verra bien in English.
  ISBN 978-1-60235-283-4 (pbk. : alk. paper) -- ISBN 978-1-60235-284-1 (ebook)
  I. McGookey, Kathleen. II. Title.

PQ2613.O22O5713 2012
841'.914--dc23

                                            2011053119

Cover design by David Blakesley.
Cover image by Georges L. Godeau.

Printed on acid-free paper.

Parlor Press, LLC is an independent publisher of scholarly and trade titles in print and multimedia formats. This book is available in paperback and ebook formats from Parlor Press on the World Wide Web at http://www.parlorpress.com or through online and brick-and-mortar bookstores. For submission information or to find out about Parlor Press publications, write to Parlor Press, 3015 Brackenberry Drive, Anderson, South Carolina, 29621, or e-mail editor@parlorpress.com.

Contents

Acknowledgments vii

Goosebumps 3

Peasants 5
She Clings to Herself 6
The Saint-Antoine Inn 7
Ninny 8
The Nurse 9
Dance Number 10
Tortebresse 11
Bus Trip 12
The Goalie 13
At the School in Town 14
Ribiera 15
Curtain 16

Norway 17

The Ruhr River Valley 19
Lubeck 20
Buffet 21
The Japanese 22
Fascination 23
A Night on Board 24
The Hospital 25
Photo 26
The Old Folks 27
Bergen 28
On the Whole 29

A Scottish Woman 31

Della 33
Juggling 34
Waiting 35
Panic 36
Like a Trophy 37
Happy 38
A Character 39
The Heart 40
Fort Foucault 41

From Time to Time 43

The Brickmaker 45
The Laundromat at Saint-Jean 46
The Rut 47
Illusions 48
Animals 49
Electricity 50
The Hairdresser 51
Joelle 52
Decree 53
The Briant Fiefdom 54
Flood Level 55
Reunion 56
Simone 57
Intuition 58
The Best Is 59
Residence Under Surveillance 60
A Good Citizen 61
"Listen to the Bird" 62

A Russian Guide   63
Soliloquy   64
Paradise   65
Mr. Jean Rostand   66

In Season   69

Sister Jeanne   71
The Little String   72
The Poet   73
The House with the Windmill   74
Alice   75
Tough Old Chap   76
One Hundred Degrees Celsius   77
Gallo-Roman Site   78
Horses   79
The Mound of the Alder Tree   80
Perplexity   81
Place Saint-Jean   82
In the Month of August   83
Gwen   84
A Festive Evening   85
God Arthur   86
Meadowsweet   87
Le Roman de Renart   88
Anonymity   89
"Our Property" (H.M.)   90
I Revise   91
Tourism   92
The Rose Garden   93
Always Himself   94
Absentmindedness   95

Georges Mounin 97

Meeting 99
Transformation 100
In Clotet 101
Loyalty 102
The Subject 103
Mecca 104
Olympus 105
Music 106
Shirt Open 107
Cemetery 108
A Dream 109

About the Author 111
About the Translator 113
Free Verse Editions 115

Acknowledgments

Acknowledgment is made to the following journals, where these translations were first published:

AGNI Online: "Gallo-Roman Site," "A Russian Guide," "Illusions," "Gwen," "Paradise,"
The Antioch Review: "Tortebresse"
Basalt: "Sister Jeanne"
Burnside Review: "Photo," "The Laundromat at Saint-Jeanne"
Chase Park: "The Japanese," "Della," "Waiting," "Joelle," "Like a Trophy," "Absentmindedness," "The Poet," "Anonymity"
Circumference: "Place Saint-Jean," "Transformation," "Tourism"
Connecticut Review: "Flood Level," "The Little String," "Dance Number"
Current Accounts: "Cemetery," "A Dream," "Mecca," "Shirt Open," "Music"
Denver Quarterly: "Horses," "In the Month of August," "The Rose Garden," "Alice"
Diner: "Panic"
Five Fingers Review: "Bergen," "The Nurse," "Ruhr River Valley," "The Saint-Antoine Inn"
Free Verse: "The Goalie," "The Briant Fiefdom," "Reunion," "Listen to the Bird," "Soliloquy," "Mr. Jean Rostand," "God Arthur," "Le Roman de Renart," "Meeting," "In Clotet," "The Subject," "Olympus"
Great River Review: "The Hairdresser," "Intuition" (as "Discrimination")
Hawai'i Review: "The Best Is," "Meadowsweet"
Indiana Review: "Juggling," "Happy"
Interlochen Review: "One Hundred Degrees Celsius"
jubilat: "Curtain"

The MacGuffin: "The Heart," "Fascination"
The Marlboro Review: "Electricity," "The Mound of the Alder Tree"
Meridian: "The House with the Windmill," "Simone," "Lubeck"
Mid-American Review: "Animals"
Natural Bridge: "Loyalty," "At the Hospital"
Phoebe: "Perplexity"
Poetry International: "I Revise"
Quarter After Eight: "Ninny" (as "Clasp"), "Our Property,"
River City: "Tough Old Chap"
Rhino: "On the Whole"
Salt Hill: "The Brickmaker"
Stand: "A Night on Board," "The Old Folks" (as "My Parents"), "At the School in Town," "She Clings To Herself," "Always Himself"
Sonora Review: "Fort Foucault"
Spoon River Poetry Review: "A Good Citizen"
Willow Springs: "Buffet"

My deepest thanks to Jim Murphy, who read early drafts of these translations and corrected my mistakes. Jim, without you, this book wouldn't exist. My gratitude also to both Dr. Anne Larsen and Valérie Rouzeau, who gave generously of their time and expertise, and to Louis Dubost, for his assistance and enthusiasm for this project.

WE'LL SEE

Goosebumps

4

Peasants

    Ever since she was little, her mother would take her along to sell the produce from the farm. They would walk with their load, ten kilometers, whether it rained or the wind blew. At noon, the baskets empty, they would go into a bistro, always the same one, to have a snack, at a table with a cloth. There was a little money left. Sometimes none. But they had lunched in town, like two ladies.

She Clings to Herself

Her husband is dead, her married children live far away. In her big house, she is afraid of noises, she takes refuge in town at other peoples' houses, she travels. Coming home in the evening is anguish. In winter, she knits in front of the tv, she takes sleeping pills. At dawn, she runs to the mailbox. The paper is there. The world is still there.

The Saint-Antoine Inn

Sometimes, when the chef surpasses himself, when the door in back opens like that of matadors in amphitheaters, when the waiters enter with their bedecked trays and subtle smells, all talk stops, the faces prepare themselves for a huge feast.

Here, you don't throw yourself at the food, you smell it, you contemplate it at length before unfolding your napkin in homage to the master of this victory, who has come out of his kitchen for the moment of silence.

Ninny

She's a little old woman, like a feather. She has dug hard to find the cesspool, she has joked with the men who emptied it and now she wants to put the plug back in but it's too heavy, she is out of breath. And night is coming. Behind his hedge, her young neighbor understands. He comes over, simply by chance, with a tool, and the cover, obedient, fits in snugly.

Providence has blue eyes.

The Nurse

She quit her job to go to Sudan and help Doctors Without Borders. When they were gone, she took care of the sick people who lined up. Yesterday, she came home to earn enough money to pay her rent and buy another plane ticket. A kind of splendor lights her gaze as if she were writing a beautiful poem.

Dance Number

I am the only spectator at this circus with four hundred sheep. The shepherd, aside, mutters. His six dogs listen, divide the commands, and the herd, like a snake, glides between the fields. Not an ear of corn stolen. Their objective is farther away, a piece of fallow land. Behind the sheep, the man walks. To applaud would disturb him.

Tortebresse

The farm burned that night. In the stable, the man counts the dead: ten burned cows. While the meadows are still so beautiful! It's spring and the smoke that rises from the debris vanishes slowly like a funeral. The herds that slept outside are still standing. The odor curdles their milk.

Bus Trip

There were forty of them, they came from far away to gather flowers and one of them just died in the restaurant. The firemen, the doctor, squeeze into the doorway. Outside, curious onlookers await the body. Stretched out in the aisle, it has time. The pale waitresses step over it. To stumble with the dinners would be tragic. Because of the laughter.

The Goalie

The best, he came to win the cup and lost it on a fluke. With his head in his hands, he hears the cheers that aren't for him and suddenly, twenty years old, he decides to get mixed up with the crowd, he approaches all the people standing, he bows to them as best he can to thank them, and he stands there, without the cup; so little, but so big.

At the School in Town

The children of the village are early risers. They emerge from all the streets and wait for the bus. With the girls on one side and the boys on the other, they form two rows for telling secrets. Then when everything is said, they lean against the wall with a book or a cigarette. The day advances. Let each have his own.

Ribiera

In the sun, in the clearing, with his six houses, his sleeping herd, his piles of wood, of stones, his vipers, and the mild breeze that rummages up there in the trees.

Sitting on the threshold of the temple, I am two thousand years younger and the gods have all agreed in order to please me.

Curtain

One day I will fall into a sunken road, far from everything. My dog will laugh and then, seeing me asleep, he will lie down to do the same. I don't know when my silence will worry him and what he will do. He is a black and secretive beast.

Norway

The Ruhr River Valley

On the highway, semis are lined up. In each cab, a man: young, old, hairy, bald, dreamy, cheerful, his hands flat on the wheel, then elbows, then a finger. He admires the frisky bus that passes. One day, he will ride inside, without the steering wheel, head empty. But for now, he is there, he drives, he unloads, lies down, sleeps, fills it up, and leaves. In two days, the weekend. A mouthful of bread.

Lubeck

The Buddenbrocks, Thomas Mann. He has maybe run on this sidewalk. I look for his house. Forty years already that he has been dead. Even the cemetery would leave me cold. The street sweepers go away, the women run. A policeman is interested in me. I look at my watch and enter the train station. Four burly men wait for me. I look for a German newspaper. No matter what I do, I'm not from here.

Buffet

In Copenhagen, at the buffet, spoils. On three levels, the French fill their plates with multi-colored food, then disengage themselves and rush to their tables to devour it, sweltering, and then, as soon as the mood passes, do it all again. If you are not big and strong, you will not get the grilled salmon. A froggish woman has pulled it off: her plate is full of seafood. In my plate: misery.

I waited out the general looting, I had coffee and, finally alone, I returned to the feast. There were some pink shrimp left. I took them all.

The Japanese

    Wearing jeans, badly made up and disheveled, they are everywhere, they take photos, they move in a flock, like starlings.
    At noon, they invade the buffet, they sneak in under your arms, between your legs, they are in front, they choose their food, vanish, beat you to the tables, take the places facing the sky, the ocean, they ignore you, talking among themselves, a lot, and loudly, they are happy to be there, the boat belongs to them.
    The following morning, they have left, you breathe and that night when you arrive at your hotel, three hundred kilometers away, two buses have preceded you. Theirs.

Fascination

On the cruise ship, caught in the gleam of the jewelry department, she is alone with her smiling arms. No, she doesn't want anything. Slender in her dress without pockets or tools, she contemplates the sparkling stones. There are the same ones in Tokyo. But there, she runs away, she is shut away. Here, she is free.

When I walked by again, she was still there, outside of time.

A Night on Board

They responded when their names were called, they went to their cabin, tried the beds and the faucets, and then, reassured, they go round to the decks, stairways, and wind. The wake captivates them. Soon, dinner. While waiting, they look for a place at the small tables where no one is drinking. Those who are standing contemplate the sunset on the ocean. So far from home! On so much water! At their age. Too late.

The Hospital

When Madeleine fell, I lifted her up and she was covered in blood.
The doctors, in the ambulance, spoke Norwegian.
At the hospital, a woman told her in French, "Broken arm—sew up the forehead."
Two hours later, she left with her head bandaged, her arm in a sling.
Speed, skill, and gentleness: almost a love story.

Photo

There is a young elk, on the end of a thin rope, at the edge of the road, close to a hut where a woman sells animal skins. The buses stop for the photo. The absolute best is to take the animal by the neck and smile at the lens. Behind: mountains, a stream. Sometimes the animal bucks and throws itself to the ground. It is wasting its time and strength because the tourists have driven two thousand kilometers for it. And they must have the photo of the elk before returning home.

The Old Folks

They are living, they have faces, hands, ideas, they compete to say them, to hear the responses, to make us laugh. In the morning, they get up the earliest, they take showers, they pack their suitcases, they are the first people in the restaurant, their eyes glitter, they select the sweetmeats, and with their arms full, they go to sit at their table, serious. They even fill their pockets with bread to throw to the seagulls on the sun deck. They amuse themselves like children when the birds come to their hands.

Bergen

It is raining. The local guide proposes going down to the harbor, despite everything. "With umbrellas." No one has one. In that case, the maritime museum. The tourists meddle with the anchors, sit on the ships' beams, yawn.

At last, the young woman mentions Hamsun, "A great artist." I state my opinion, "Except that he went astray, like Napoleon, Nietzsche." Her eyes light up; she has so many things to say about that. Me too. My fellow travelers: nothing at all. They are the majority.

On the Whole

Norway is a mountainous country. Everywhere, spring waters. Fisherman, I dream of casting my line. But the salmon laugh. To fish here, you need a line so thin you can't see it. And the maps are exorbitantly priced.

The Norwegians make their living from the woods, the ocean, the oil. Those who have nothing at all live off that anyway. They sit on the sidewalks and watch the bicycle races while music plays. They have sandwiches and good seats. They even seem happy. Happiness here smells like the grass.

A Scottish Woman

Della

She is a photographer. On assignment in France to photograph four writers, she takes pictures of them at their houses, in the bog, the water towers, an ultralight plane. In which she goes up. She is in love with the pilot. But he is married. Too bad.

She eats once a day. She whiles away the night like an ogre, with whiskey and tobacco, and develops her film. In the morning, she can't get over how beautiful her pictures are.

At the market, she buys a rabbit. For fun. Because she's going home to Scotland soon, she asks me if I want it. I accept, then I suggest she offer it to someone else. Her gaze blackens. "You've changed your mind?" I suffer for three seconds. Behind the house, a box of dandelions awaits it. The rabbit amuses itself in it. We were cold.

Juggling

In her rough voice, she makes an appointment. She is on time. First, she drinks three whiskeys while talking poetry, then she has a snack. Suddenly, she gets up and hangs up a black curtain, opens a white umbrella and makes me sit on a footstool. There, I must dream that I throw some balls, again and again with each hand like Chaplin in The Dictator. With elegance, and smiling if possible. At seventy years old, I obey. With each toss that she likes, I receive a compliment. Like at the circus.

Waiting

All by yourself, you fill the house with your shouts, your laughs, and your light.

In the evening, when you go away, we drift, the silence makes our heads spin. We sleep like logs and the next day we ask ourselves what in the world we did to make you leave. For three days, an eternity. Elsewhere, you sow the same seeds and we are jealous of the people who welcome you.

They release you and you arrive in "Your Clio" with a smile as wide as your windshield.

And we are healed.

Panic

Like a well-behaved child, she examines my friend's paintings. Patiently she listens, asks questions. There is yet the ultralight plane, for which she has come. The apparatus coughs, then takes off lamely and fades away.

On the ground, in the icy wind, I fantasize, I see bodies, the police, the family. And then, behind, in the sky, a fly grows larger. Arms raised, I talk to myself.

Like a Trophy

I show you the most beautiful water tower that I constructed and you stamp your foot for us to stop. We unpack the equipment and, with your feet on the ground, you get to work.

You don't have a coat or a jacket, and the winter wind tries to tear away the rest. You laugh, because in your country it's even colder, and because you still have pictures to take. We have, nevertheless, an appointment, but you are deaf. "It's the most beautiful work of art, not to be missed."

In your makeshift lab, you spend the night with it and the next day you can't find the words to thank me.

Me too.

Happy

Hawk-eyed, I visit your remote region. It is a rocky spot, with fresh running streams and flowers. And a bed of moss on which you dream of changing the world. Demanding, you cannot be stopped when you want something. Disarming, you dissolve rocks and your charm does the rest.

Your friend, "the intolerant one," with the big stomach is happy. Your stomach is flat and one against another they make a totem pole.

A Character

You forget what I give you, poems, books, pictures, but you remember three grasses that aren't like the others in the back of the swamp. And you know the trail to see them again, you charm the boatman to go back there and the two of you arrive at just the spot, right at the violet-colored tuft at the foot of an ash tree. You get down and you wait until nothing moves to photograph it.

The man wonders who you are. Alone with you in the jungle, he gets ideas. But the risks are great: in winter, one can see through the trees from far away. And you can yell. Thoughtful, he grips his oar again, to earn his tip.

The Heart

Sorceress, daughter of a Viking, of the Loch Ness monster, with your way of walking like a shepherdess, your flowing mane of dirty blonde hair, you know how to do everything and when you come to my friend's house, my friend the commanding officer of a ship, lumberjack, artist, and collector of Brazilian butterflies, when you demand permission to photograph his father's forge, the geraniums and a shirt hung in the sun, I no longer know you. Reserved, you contemplate paintings from top to bottom of the house, wiping dust and spiders away with your finger, and you humbly follow this great man, old oak, saint, even god, who is starting to fall in love with you at two thousand kilometers an hour like in his airplane.

I'm not rich, but I would give a great deal for you to stay here until the end of time and marry him. I would come back now and then for a crumb. You would have so much that no one would notice it.

Fort Foucault

She stays in town in the artist's hotel. All the young people wait on her. They carry her materials, they fear her, they admire her. At night, she returns late. In her room, disorder reigns. She likes this. On her unmade bed, she breathes for a moment, then gets set up to print her pictures. Anxiously she shows them to me. I recognize myself in magic spells. One day, everything will be shown in Edinburgh, Aberdeen, la Rochelle. Friends will see me. They will shake their heads. "So, I will never be serious!"

February 8, 1993

From Time to Time

The Brickmaker

The brickmaker demanded twenty kilowatts. His diesel kiln is worn out. The planning commission foresaw the death of the little brickmakers. I am burdened with the execution.

The man protests. He makes the best tiles because of the way they are baked. He opens the window. "Look! We monitor the color!" It's true. I watched the tiles blaze. And the man's gaze.

I lost. I proposed a reprieve. On exceptional grounds.

The Laundromat at Saint-Jean

Don't look for flowers in the window, they don't grow there.
In the pressing room, the machines hammer their heads, push down their chests. The steam burns them. And the boss raises up a help wanted sign.
I carry out, under my arm, dry laundry that smells like violets. It is white like the hands of a dead woman.

The Rut

Water rises in the cornfield. The peasants consult the sky. Hurry.

They worked hard but the burden is heavy and the wheels sink. Mud splashes up in their faces. Push. The tractor comes out into the road.

The master goes back to the mire. He plunges his pitchfork in. The rain glazes his shoulders. They no longer have shoulders. They look at the rut. They think about the last trip.

Illusions

We each have our own way of loving unhappy people.
You, you walk with him, you talk with him about his misery, together you build better days to come.
Me, I love her, I can't do anything else.
But we must keep up our illusions. They are life.

Animals

Soon, morning over the swamp. Beautiful peaches are born in the dawn.

I am a regular. Because I walk so often in the undergrowth, I no longer crash into dead trees and the peaceful herds have adopted me. They confuse me with the trees.

A heifer close to the river. I caress her rump in passing. She presses her neck on my leg, then she follows me into the ash trees. From time to time, I murmur a word. She shakes her ear. It is our code.

Electricity

Like a little sun, a bulb was turned on under the black beams. The peasant who was having lunch stood up, then took off his hat. The children clapped and the sick woman in the alcove sat down, in her bed jacket, to take part.

The man in the varnished shoes who pushed the button remains dumbfounded. This is not called for in his job.

Chantermerle, 1960

The Hairdresser

Suzy is the best hairdresser in the salon. Silently, she cuts, rolls, combs, and concentrates.

In her armchair, Madame is astonished: "They say she creates?"

It's true that Madame is a regular at art exhibitions. But her hair isn't a canvas. Painting is an art, hairdressing is a trade.

Madame is always right.

Joelle

They call me Yoyo. I take what I'm given.

Ever since my father got sick, my mother went crazy and my big sister makes the rules. Me, I do the dishes and my homework when I have the time.

On Sundays, I go to the hospital with my mother. After the first moment, I sit on the floor and read romance novels. At school, I'm two years behind and later, I'm going to be a cleaning woman. In books, the maids sometimes meet men who love them. And they are happy.

Decree

It is a letter from the Minister to his deputies. It contains an order, a suggestion. Those who hate orders take it for a suggestion. They file it and continue to read the newspaper.

The others who suffer from lethargy seize the opportunity. They open the windows, tip up the tables and draw up the plans for future water towers. They telephone the villages to announce the news.

When the documents are finally ready, when only a stamp is needed to launch everything, a leaflet arrives that suspends the funds. The windows are closed. In armchairs, intestines ferment, heads are sick.

The best ones only work, generally, ten or so times in their careers. Afterwards, they join erudite groups to file, every six months, a footnoted report on the evolution of the wheelbarrow in the region, from its origins to our days.

The Briant Fiefdom

1945

Herds grazed during the summer at the Briant Fiefdom.

One day, soldiers chased them away. They made a camp there. Women marched in a row. In the summer, they grazed; in the winter, they died.

Passengers on the trains bound for Paris opened their windows when the trains reached the camp. They said, "Jews."

Peace was restored. But at the Briant Fiefdom, the shepherd refuses to leave. The earth is red and the dog howls at death. So the master sowed some wheat. It grows thickly.

Flood Level

There is always a Popof dog, a Socrates dog, dinner at seven o'clock, the second sitting, pretty bathrooms, "please, do!" and native women to tell you the weather will be beautiful soon.

There is always the house cocktail bar at the pool's edge, the copper smiles, and on the way, a donation box for change for those poor asses, those poor arabs.

It begins to get shitty in the end.

Reunion

Nature, here I am finally at your disposal. For the forty years that they've held me, I hardly knew where I was, I needed to walk on your paths, in your fields, in your streams. They have occasionally changed places but I would recognize your sun, your wind and soon, if you want, I will take your arm again to go with you into the depths where you were teaching me your language, do you remember, it was summer, the peasants were napping: generous, you offered me the best of you that we admired with a magnifying glass, head to head, like two lovers. We were, I was ten years old and you, you've never said it.

1981

Simone

She was the girl of the café. On the bench, outside, she told me about her affairs with the blacksmith; I told her about mine with her cousin. With her pretty figure and smile, I often led the dancing with her. Spinning tops, we closed our eyes. The bravos would awaken us like the morning after a beautiful night. The blacksmith made us pay for it during the week.

Intuition

When I was a student, my father earned little, my mother worked hard. At noon, on a bench, I ate for a franc.

Today, I am a professor and at Easter, I invite them to a good restaurant to eat. The large woman who dines near us sizes us up and ruffles her feathers. We must have made a mistake with the menu.

The Best Is

to admire, to be lost in. It can happen that despite this, you receive some blows: don't return them, don't ask for explanations, for help, don't whine or sneer. Hold your tongue. Keep your distance, do your utmost to help, serve, without hope of repayment. Finally, drown yourself alone. To pay for your funeral in advance is good planning.

Residence Under Surveillance

They are the Regional Administrator, the Captain of Police, and the Chief of Police. They don't torture me all the time, one day they decide to visit my establishment, they warn me about the date, they arrive on time, they knock, they don't say, "You're the one who writes poems and protests in the newspapers," but, "You're the one, the water, the electricity." While I search for words, they photograph the tables and the walls. They don't find horses here, or mountains, or postcards, or naked women like at my neighbors' houses, but unfinished drawings, face down, which confirm my guilt. Happy, they rub their hands together, glance outside to fool me, and leave sending me a sign, click of handcuffs.

1979

A Good Citizen

I have a pair of gray trousers, a striped shirt and when I can, I walk to work. A senior banking executive, I earn thirty thousand dollars per year, that's how much we need to live well. Sundays, with the children, we go to the country, we eat outside, we take pictures. While they sleep I read the paper, I assure myself that my country is still the most powerful in the world. It's normal because the subsoil is rich and our people are courageous, inventive, and free. If one day a country takes us to war, we will win. But is all this true? Of course it is.

1980

"Listen to the Bird"

Disruption of the senses. On stage, they mime a pretty story. The music helps them. A woman who is almost nude sings. A thousand people wonder. Still, the message is clear, the poetry as well.

In the audience, an important man protests: "They don't know how to move!" Of course! It's beautiful for exactly that reason.

A Russian Guide

She is twenty, wears jeans, and up there, she sleeps like a log, like Natacha Rostov. She doesn't know anything about her, she refuses to talk about Russian writers. Besides, since they don't belong to me, she is willing to loan them because I have paid, to extricate herself. She keeps her distance, I help her liberate herself, I walk alone on Russian soil in the footsteps of the great men I love. They are there, I saw their statues, their houses, their cemetery. That must suffice.

Soliloquy

    Char is eighty years old. He was my friend, he wrote that to me. I believed him.

    Today he is alive and silent, despite four calls, I remember his table overloaded with unopened letters. We had coffee on them. He said, "I dream of friends who wouldn't wait for a response."

    I am his friend and I wait. Except if he is turned against the wall.

1987

Paradise

Paradise is an island in the sun. Golden grapes ripen in the grass. Soft music floats. Everywhere, transparent beings.

In this country without roads, without cars, without offices, without factories, well-being is foreseen. It doesn't wear itself out.

But only the soul is concerned, that little bird that lives in us which we never see. Like God.

It is a world of valuable substances for the philosophers amiss in their reasoning.

Maupassant said that the invisible exists and that man doesn't have the necessary equipment to see it.

August 13, 1973
Mr. Jean Rostand
of the French Academy

Dear Mr. Rostand,

I wake from a dream which I share with you:
You live in an old house with a gate that opens on the road. With my wife, I enter, cross the courtyard, and enter a room on street level. In the middle, a big bed, a violet eiderdown. We are going to leave when someone comes in and murmurs, "He's there, he's dying." I turn around, raise myself on my tiptoes and I see you, very much lost in lace like Louis XV. Your face is swollen, eyes closed, and it looks like it's all over when suddenly you move, the eiderdown slides off and you sit up, you want to get up. And that's just what you do. Your face changes, you are better quickly, and I approach you with my wife, so close that you see us and I fall on my knees, without saying hello properly. You understand right away what this is about and you place your hand on my head in asking me to stand up. You choose an old armchair for yourself and offer us chairs. And you want to know. I tell you that as I was passing, the desire to come and chat a little overtook me. About Jaures Medvedev's book. *Lyssenko's Grandeur and Fall* and some of your own, one of which was *A Short History of Biology*. I slyly point out that you didn't cite Lyssenko in your own. You smile like on the cover of *At The Boundaries of the Superhuman*, with the frog, and respond that with Lyssenko, it was quite the opposite. Then we talk about your work which I know by heart since I read it all straight through one winter.

It's at this moment that neighborhood women—well-endowed—come in with their children and all of them surround you to kiss you. You willingly surrender to their outpouring. In your enthusiasm, you kiss us as well and tell them that we are friends. Many of them are relatives, and since they make themselves comfortable, you get up, go out in the courtyard, take me by the arm and gently ask me to bring you Medvedev's book. I don't dare think you don't know about it. Nevertheless, I make a note of it and you give me your identification cards to deliver to Estate Management. Meanwhile, your chauffeur brings the car around. You are now wearing a black coat, a round hat, and your usual mustache and you decide to go out. The car starts. Like DeGaulle, you signal from behind the window to everyone there who loves you. And all disappear in a crowded narrow street.

In Season

Sister Jeanne

She is old, she has all the illnesses and in her armchair she watches the summer pass. Another one.

At noon, when she can't stand it any longer, she lifts her arm and calls Jeanne, like herself, over there in her chair. "So? How's the weather? The family? The pain?" "The same." After that, silence settles in, the bill adds up. Each one sleeps in her own way.

The Little String

The little unbreakable string, always in tune, hidden in my pocket for fifty years, still works. Every three months, it wakes up, alerts me that it is there and that if I'm up to it, it can. Despite my age, I roll up my sleeves and we spend the day together. It is generous. By nightfall, I am dead.

The Poet

The library security guard is twenty years old. He is tall and blond like a poplar and his eyes are pieces of the sky. Today, he couldn't restrain himself; "Are you the poet?" I shrugged my shoulders and replied, "Like you, like everyone." He blushed to say there were big and little poets.

We agreed that there are only poets, nothing more, and ever since then, I've had a friend in that place.

The House with the Windmill

They didn't hide behind the curtains to spy on us, see how we looked, how we were dressed, if we had been drinking, or if we seemed gentle or austere.

As soon as they saw the car, they came out on the gravel, the parents and their four children just barely awake, and we didn't know where to start, who to kiss, whose hand to shake and thank for their hospitality, we mingled with them.

It was winter. Time to sit down, chat with each person, eat; the day unraveled like a luxury train driving away. Already time to leave. Talking about it makes it seem real.

Alice

It's our first visit. From the beginning, she chooses me. Her pretty face lights up, and, quite naturally she approaches, she spots my hearing aid; for ten seconds, she considers it. Then she prattles with my glass, she leans on my knee, she takes a piece of paper and draws. I watch and also roughly sketch a little man. She laughs and adopts me for life. With her parents' permission, because she is two years old and I am seventy.

Tough Old Chap

Gray mammoth, he emerges on a lane between two high banks, he almost touches the branches, with his arms and wheels, then the task done, he takes care of the tractor, covered with clay that falls on each trip around, big clods the size of a dog, and up there, the man who is wound up, covered, shaken on the machine, comes near, passes in misery, a green skeleton who winks and smiles because he has recognized me, fifty years since I've been here, the two of us in an open bog, winter, a storm, and there is nothing else.

One Hundred Degrees Celsius

The house next door is silent. The children's backyard is empty. Yesterday, the little girl was scalded. At the hospital, they pulled off her skin to put on new skin. Her mother is with her. In the evening, the father comes home, somber.

The little girl comes home. Seated on the balcony, she doesn't move. Her gaze is black and steady. She refuses to show her legs. "Later."

They should all go on vacation. To the lake. To rest and bathe. Children love water. The mother, who spilled the milk, carries a weight.

Gallo-Roman Site

Each excavation, a story. The people who once lived there worked, ate, bathed, and slept. In the evening, some of them went out to lie in the grass and look at the clouds that passed, tore each other to pieces and were reborn. The sun god set, another sometimes rose and millions of fires lit up around it. Nothing fell. Man thought the world was beautiful and to live in it was worth the sorrow.

Horses

The three horses who occupy this field have their routine. In the morning, they graze on thin grass. At noon, they sleep in the back part behind the nettles. Later, they look for small pools in the brook and roll to scratch themselves. In the evening, they gather under the poplars near the road, they listen for the men's last noises. Then night comes. From time to time, they rise to warm themselves and sneeze. From their nostrils comes a cloud that puzzles the moon.

The Mound of the Alder Tree

The little blue roads float on ten meters of mud and the overburdened workmen sink into it. The tourists curse the holes that the peasants end up filling to get their cattle trucks through. When everyone leaves and silence falls, the otters stroll and chat on the asphalt. Heron, I'm listening. These are brave people who don't speak badly of anyone.

Perplexity

Baptiste the bricklayer is old, he travels with a group. Like the others, he buys a postcard with mountains and lakes for his nephew. Telling him he loves him lacks style. And whether to sign Uncle or Baptiste . . . The man makes the sign of the cross while shaking his head.

Place Saint-Jean

In this well-situated pharmacy, without customers, I hold out my prescription and count the druggist's short-necked bottles. The bookkeeper smiles, the woman filling the prescription makes a mistake, and the apprentice hides. The boss who enters, obsequious, greets me. He judges my looks which don't please him. I look for a handkerchief in my pocket. A cloud passes. No, I don't have a gun. I simply take care of my business.

In the Month of August

Those who don't go to the ocean, to the mountains, or to Paris have ten francs in their pockets. They hold the coin for entering the pool tightly in their hands.

To put their shorts, their sandals in a locker, they need another coin. But to have one coin every day is already an extravagance.

In the water, all this isn't obvious.

Gwen

A half-century separates us. Saturday, when I bring you to my studio with your yellow hair and backpack, you tell me about your week and at dinner you drink three liters of water and talk to me about Kant as if you had been at war with him. Sometimes, I don't agree, you show your claws and push them in me. You're called the Egyptian because of your dark complexion and almond eyes. You are a beautiful girl, the daughter of your father, my friend, and I could be his father. These are fragile matters, properly handled with caution and love, so they will last.

A Festive Evening

The surgeon that everyone knows introduced the Prefect's wife to me. Young and beautiful, she prides herself on her knowledge of literature. We talked for a long time. She gave me her address so she could receive my book.

I saw her again six months later at an exhibition. Her cheeks on fire, she kissed me to excuse her silence. She left her hand on my arm. My lofty age chirped.

God Arthur

When I tell Louis that his painting takes wing, free, and sways, and that he is a child, he smiles with pride but when I add that nothing exists without wild excess, he thinks this over and gives me the cold shoulder.

And still, how can one walk up there without being a little crazy or crippled? I've spent my life there.

Meadowsweet

They live in flocks under the trees, they are taller than I am, they bend when I approach and caress me with their blond curls. Their strange scent follows you, overtakes you, even intoxicates you after some time. The peasants who've known them forever call them the queens of the meadows, because of their use in herbal tea.

Le Roman de Renart

They rehearsed all winter, the girls, the boys, and in the spring they performed the farce in the Protestant church. For fifty people, their families.

They weren't any less happy, they jumped in the stalls, leapt up again, rolled on the ground with laughter, and charged about, howling like wolves.

When the play finished, breathless, they mingled with the public, not for praise, but to offer each person their surplus of joy.

Outside was the weather of the twenty-first century. To return home was a burden.

Anonymity

One day, I wished for anonymity for my poems, so that they would go out alone. In the shadows, I dreamed.
But since they dragged their feet, I went out and walked in front. No good.
From then on, at my house, we all sit down. The weather is fine. We cook crepes and we don't expect anyone.

"Our Property" (H.M.)

Here, I own ten thousand hectares of meadows, trees, and rivers. The peasants who repair the fences and pay the taxes respect me. They ask me if the fishing is good and when I sit down on a tree trunk they sit beside me for a moment. We speak the same language and of the same things without effort.

In winter, when the beasts and men vanish, I walk my land alone.

I Revise

I revise six poems in the time it takes a woman to arrange her hair: a lock here, another there, I look at them in the mirror and when nothing surpasses them, or a strand peeks out as a surprise, I take them out into the street, I see right away whether I've been glanced at.

Time passes quickly; one day, they will be white and I will be nothing more than their only friend.

Tourism

Eclache, a village at high elevation. Forests cut it off from the world. In the main road, cow-dung. Two dogs sleep in the middle of it. A rooster watches over them. Lower down, a chapel like a jewel. Women who were chatting hide. Vanish.

The Rose Garden

It is a retirement home in a remote spot. A door with a window is anticipated in order to watch the cows in the meadow. Far away, a bridge towards the sea.

On Sunday, families come to take their relatives out. Those who are left gather in the game room, near the dining room. On the wall, the evening menu: soup, blanquette with white sauce, crème caramel. At four o'clock, a girl pushes a tea cart. In a hallway, a door gapes open to show a gray face. Behind it, a little bed, like a catafalque.

This establishment is new. It is one of the best of its kind.

Always Himself

The more my father aged, the more he climbed on the vine-props to move from meadow to meadow. He stood up there, and the more I begged him to come down—I hid my eyes—the more he laughed and gestured. He stuck out his red tongue and joked: "I don't know what I can die of!" Already, he had no more than half a lung. But a blacksmith's bellows, without a doubt.

Absentmindedness

This morning while I was strolling, the weather was so beautiful that I rang at the prison, I asked for Georges Godeau. The guard checked his list but didn't see that name. He was going to look again when I told him that it was me, sentenced for life for having written too many books. The man understood my problem right away. Long ago, he showed me in through the bars. I'm always here.

Georges Mounin

Meeting

One day, a Belgian friend confided to me that at a banquet, in Knokke, he found himself facing Georges Mounin, a man like Homer, Ulysses, and that he lived in Aix-en-Provence.

We took the road South. While we were looking for the street, a passerby approached: it was Georges Mounin. He had just written me for the first time. He kept us two hours. After, under the plane trees, I wanted to climb trees. Upon my return, a message waited for me: "I was without a doubt a fine man, but I had everything to learn."

Thirty-five years later, he is dead. Everything I've learned fits in the hollow of my hand. "Show me," he used to say.

Transformation

I've felt the wind, I've worked, suffered, I've understood. He wrote me: "And now it so happens that your poems exist . . . Too bad that Niort is so far away."

I couldn't throw myself in the river, I didn't have a gun. I took my cap and simply walked in the countryside. The maples, the ashes, were olive trees and the peasants Homer, Ulysses. I was in Greece.

In Clotet

When he was young, he had thrown himself into politics. To change the world. But the world was fine the way it was. Then, he studied to become a professor. Of linguistics. To understand poetry better. In fact, to be happy. That he was, for forty years in spite of the defeats. For him, they were victories.

In his ancient house, he gardened. He didn't fire guns into the air to terrorize the neighbors. On the contrary, he approached his iron fence, gathered the raspberries which hung over, and slipped them to the children through the fence, along with his voice, full of music.

The poetry he loved didn't go away.

Loyalty

He had a gang to seize the Citadel. There were fifteen of us, agreed on everything. But from the top of its walls, the Citadel laughed, threw us back with its pikes.

He lifted our spirits, he said that the tunnel was long but what a light at the end! Some no longer believed it. They chose another side, another leader who was already in the castle.

Those who remained sat around a water whose brilliance transforms.

The Subject

He had never written a single line of poetry but he knew thousands. He had to be coaxed to recite from some. "Badly, like everyone," he said.

For thirty years, I sent him my poems. He underlined one, two, and as for the others, he wrote: "They don't speak to me, I don't know why," or "Here is the real mistake that lies in wait for you." The worst was his silence.

He claimed that a poet writes between one and three dozen fine texts in his life. Final judgement.

Mecca

In the morning, we would leave to walk in the fields. When the sun grew hot, he used to take his shirt off and his hairy torso shone brightly. He used to smack himself and we would quicken our pace out of hunger, because a stuffed rabbit awaited us. We would serve ourselves before he did and then he would take the rest; a bottle of white wine was within his reach. Like a child, he didn't have any boundaries. He used to sing, "My Normandy," because he came from there, like his father the glass-blower.

Olympus

He said to me, ". . . Then, there is always something greater than the poems one writes, it is the ones that one lives first. Nothing can replace life and, for my part, I would give one hundred printed pages signed with my name, and even distinguished by flattering book reviews for one month of life, perfectly lived."

I understood, but when I complained, in spite of everything, about the deserts, he added: "No other way than immersing yourself again in your life."

He was a war general and father of a family.

Music

Once, with his wife, they traveled across France to my region, to listen to the three thousand hens that a nephew was raising on his farm. Silent, we waited for twilight and the melody rose up. Mozart, Beethoven, Indian music? The debate began not far from there, at my father's house. A peasant, my father wasn't afraid of a scholar. He put his dialect on the table to provoke the linguist. The evening crackled.

Shirt Open

I spent two days re-reading our letters, especially his. The following day, I wandered in the garden without saying a word, without pulling a weed, without wanting to eat, drink, write, or go take a stroll. At night, I didn't sleep a wink. In the morning, I searched for him in photo albums: it was summer; shirt open, he kidded around with my dog; on the stone table, two coffees cooled; it was time for his nap.

He slept like a log to live one hundred years. We had faith in it.

Cemetery

At the Salvetat cemetery, up there, in the trees, a new stone slab: "Louis Leboucher, known as Georges Mounin." They were made to live together, without clashing but standing up. Today, now that he is laid to rest, in sunlight, his back to the mountain, I sat down on the low wall and I knocked three times with a stone. Does one ever know? He knew it.

A Dream

Louis! Get up, come out of this hole and brush off your vest. The Salvetat shopkeepers wait for us, they still have apples, good meat; I will carry the basket and you will buy *le Monde* at the tobacco shop. Then we will take the path back to Jasse, the good people at the side will greet us and we will finish the path, strolling. The weather is nice up there in the meadow. We will prop up the wobbly table to drink one whiskey, two. Ju will count them. She will glower. We will talk politics to put her off the scent.

July 22, 1993

Photograph of Georges L. Godeau. Used by permission.

About the Author

Georges L. Godeau was born in 1921 in Villiers-en-Plaine, France, and worked as an engineer, specializing in rural areas. He also devoted himself to writing; his first book was published in 1962 and he published fifteen more books before his death in 1999. Several more volumes have appeared posthumously. His work won the Prix du Livre in Poitou-Charentes in 1991. While his work has been widely translated into Japanese and Russian, English translations, aside from a few in the early seventies, have appeared only since 2001.

Godeau traveled widely during his lifetime, visiting countries including Greece, Portugal, the Soviet Union, Turkey, Morocco, Algeria, Central Asia, Czechoslavakia, Scotland, the United States, Canada, Denmark, and Norway.

A visual artist in addition to a poet, Godeau began painting in 1952. He also worked in Indian Ink. Many of his drawings and paintings appear on the covers of and throughout his books. The first exhibition of his artistic and literary work was held in 1989 in Niort, France.

"A poem should not last longer than its emotion," Godeau has said. Still, his brief prose poems capture, almost photographically, moments of everyday life. Jacques Reda has said that Godeau's poetry is poetry of "what happens when nothing happens." Others have noted that Godeau handles language with a journalistic eye, evoking daily joys and difficulties.

In his account of a day spent with Godeau, Xavier Person observed that Godeau's poems were a lot like Godeau's modest house in Magné, France—a little cold, excessively clean, very tidy, and without a lot of furniture—poems that contained only the most straightforward and impassioned elements.

About the Translator

Kathleen McGookey received both her PhD in literature with a creative dissertation and her MFA in Poetry from Western Michigan University, and her BA in French from Hope College. She received an Irving S. Gilmore Emerging Artist Grant as well as an Individual Artist grant from the Arts Fund of Kalamazoo County. For her translation of *We'll See*, she received a Hemingway grant from the French Ministry of Foreign Affairs. Her book of prose poems, *Whatever Shines*, was published by White Pine Press. Her latest work is a chapbook entitled *October Again* (2012, Burnside Review Press).

Photograph of Kathleen McGookey by Rhys VanDemark. Used by permission.

Free Verse Editions

Edited by Jon Thompson

13 ways of happily by Emily Carr
Between the Twilight and the Sky by Jennie Neighbors
Blood Orbits by Ger Killeen
The Bodies by Christopher Sindt
Child in the Road by Cindy Savett
Country Album by James Capozzi
The Curiosities by Brittany Perham
Current by Lisa Fishman
Divination Machine by F. Daniel Rzicznek
The Flying House by Dawn-Michelle Baude
Instances: Selected Poems by Jeongrye Choi, translated by Brenda
    Hillman, Wayne de Fremery, and Jeongrye Choi
A Map of Faring by Peter Riley
Physis by Nicolas Pesque, translated by Cole Swensen
Poems from above the Hill & Selected Work by Ashur Etwebi, translated by Brenda Hillman and Diallah Haidar
The Prison Poems by Miguel Hernández, translated by Michael Smith
Puppet Wardrobe by Daniel Tiffany
Quarry by Carolyn Guinzio
remanence by Boyer Rickel
Signs Following by Ger Killeen
These Beautiful Limits by Thomas Lisk
An Unchanging Blue: Selected Poems 1962–1975 by Rolf Dieter
    Brinkmann, translated by Mark Terrill
Under the Quick by Molly Bendall
Verge by Morgan Lucas Schuldt
The Wash by Adam Clay
We'll See by George Godeau, translated by Kathleen McGookey
What Stillness Illuminated by Yermiyahu Ahron Taub
Winter Journey [Viaggio d'inverno] by Attilio Bertolucci, translated
    by Nicholas Benson

CPSIA information can be obtained at www.ICGtesting.com
Printed in the USA
BVOW081855221012

303638BV00001B/6/P